CAREERS WITH THE CENTRAL INTELLIGENCE AGENCY

CIA

JUST ABOUT EVERYBODY CAN AGREE that a career with the Central Intelligence Agency sounds pretty exciting. The agency, more commonly known simply as the CIA, is the principal intelligence-gathering agency of the United States government. It is the largest and most diverse of the 17 agencies that make up the Intelligence Community, or IC, the cluster of organizations that gather and analyze classified intelligence for the federal government.

The CIA is widely known for its human intelligence mission. Human intelligence, called HUMINT, is the process of gathering and analyzing intelligence from human sources. Those sources can be operatives collecting information for the agency, or tipsters from just about anywhere who come forward to share information. Decades of movies and television have glamorized the agency's spies – officially known as "clandestine operatives" – but secret agents are actually a relatively small part of the agency's resources. The CIA employs thousands of specialists in many areas, including languages, information technology, intelligence analysis, and science and engineering, among others.

The one thing that ties together this constellation of professionals is their unwavering devotion to duty. Real life is not a movie, and working for the CIA is difficult and demanding. The agency attracts the best and brightest, and keeps them with career opportunities that are very appealing.

Everybody who works for the CIA must also pass an exhaustive background check in order to be granted a security clearance. Employees in especially sensitive positions, like clandestine operations, are required to undergo particularly rigorous investigation. To even consider a career with the CIA you must have at least a bachelor's degree or significant experience in a similar field, like the military, and a flawless personal history.

WHAT YOU CAN DO NOW

YOU CAN START PREPARING FOR your career with the CIA right now.

People who apply for jobs with the CIA generally have outstanding academic backgrounds. They have bachelor's degrees with excellent grades, speak fluently at least one foreign language and have completed an internship or two (maybe with the CIA or another IC agency). The only common exceptions to this rule are former military personnel with significant intelligence experience. A hitch in the military is an excellent way to get started on a career in the CIA.

The CIA does not operate in a vacuum. Its operations are all dictated by real-world events. Just monitor current news events around the world, and you will know what the CIA has been involved with lately. In addition, you will have a good idea of what kind of skills and knowledge the agency may be looking for. Spend at least 30 minutes every day reading up on international news.

Not all CIA employees are intelligence analysts, but it behooves you to know about the process if you plan to devote a career to the country's largest intelligence agency. Explore the websites of the various intelligence agencies to get the official version about what they do and how they do it. They will not divulge many details, of course, but at least you will get a general picture of each agency and its mission. Read books on intelligence analysis and the history of intelligence and espionage.

HISTORY OF THE CAREER

INTELLIGENCE HAS BEEN AN IMPORTANT part of international relations for thousands of years. Tribal leaders, army generals, kings, emperors, prime ministers and presidents, have all employed intelligence to gain an advantage over their adversaries. Good intelligence enables leaders to make decisions that will advance their interests in geopolitical strategy.

Intelligence gets an entire chapter in *The Art of War,* a classic text written in about 525 BC by the Chinese general Sun Tzu. In it, he says (among a great many other things that still ring true today), "If you know the enemy and know yourself, you need not fear the results of a hundred battles." *The Art of War* has been required reading for military and intelligence officers for 2500 years. If you want to learn about the history of intelligence, this book is a good place to start.

Intelligence is a force multiplier. That means that it enables conventional forces, whether political or military, to accomplish more with intelligence than they would be able to without it. For military forces, good intelligence – usually known in the field as "intel" – enables forces to target the adversary more effectively by, for example, determining where to drop one bomb to take out a specific target, rather than dropping many bombs over a large area and hoping to hit something important. You can achieve the same effect, save bombs and money, and potentially spare many innocent lives.

In politics and diplomacy, a diplomat armed with the latest intel has an advantage over a diplomat entering negotiations with minimal information. The fate of nations can rest on who has the best intelligence. "It is only the enlightened ruler and the wise general who will use the highest intelligence of the army for the purposes of spying," Sun Tzu says, "and thereby they achieve great results."

The history of American intelligence goes all the way back to the Revolutionary War. General George Washington greatly multiplied the power of his tiny Continental Army by employing spies, cryptographers, and paramilitary squads that would today be known as special forces. When he became the first President a few years later, he recommended that Congress devote money to a secret service (not the Secret Service, which was founded many years later to protect the president) to give the new government an edge in its dealings with the sophisticated governments of Europe. Did you know that Benjamin Franklin was a spy?

Both sides used intelligence during the Civil War. In fact, the North's spymaster, Allen Pinkerton, was so successful that he founded one of the world's first detective agencies after the war, the Pinkerton Agency. The company still exists today.

Military intelligence became a formal discipline in the 1880s, and grew rapidly in the early 1900s when the United States entered World War I. The period between the first and second world wars saw the United States invest heavily in cryptography capability in order to break Japanese codes.

The first civilian intelligence agency was created in 1941, and was called the Office of the Coordinator of Information. By 1942, the United States had entered World War II and the small office was replaced by the much larger Office of Strategic Services, or OSS, the forerunner of the CIA. The primary function of the OSS was to provide key decision makers with intelligence for the war effort. The OSS served as a conduit for foreign intelligence gathered by the OSS and the Federal Bureau of Investigation, and for the intelligence gathered and analyzed by the Army and Navy. The OSS was disbanded in October of 1945 after the war had been won, but was reconstituted only a few months later with the founding of the Central Intelligence Group in January 1946. In 1947 the arrangement was altered again when Congress passed the National Security Act. The act created the National Security Council and the Central Intelligence Agency.

The CIA's main mission was to coordinate the nation's intelligence activities and disseminate intelligence on matters of national security. The director of central intelligence was also named as the president's principal advisor on intelligence.

Today, the CIA is the nation's largest intelligence agency. It provides intelligence to the president and to several Congressional committees in order to keep leaders on top of the issues. It operates extremely sophisticated analysis programs and is the lead agency on all American clandestine operations. It is one of the few federal agencies whose budget is classified. The CIA has played a pivotal role in every American conflict since World War II, from going head-to-head with the Soviet KGB during the Cold War, to working alongside military personnel in Iraq and Afghanistan.

WHERE YOU WILL WORK

A CAREER WITH THE CIA CAN TAKE YOU all over the world but you will start your journey in McLean, Virginia, a small town south of Washington, DC. McLean is home to the CIA's massive headquarters campus and its training programs. The area is often referred to simply as "Langley," which was the name given to the area before the city of McLean was incorporated. If you pursue a career with the CIA or anywhere else in the Intelligence Community (IC), you will hear people say "Langley" when they mean "CIA."

Langley is just far enough outside the capital to provide a cushion from the political wrangling that goes on there. Most CIA employees and their families live near Langley. McLean and the cities surrounding it are very pleasant suburban communities, and among the few places where having a top-secret job will not make your neighbors nervous.

Many CIA employees spend their entire careers at headquarters, but many do not. They are routinely stationed at United States embassies and military bases around the world. They deploy to combat zones and often work with allied intelligence agencies. Sometimes they get to take their families with them, when they are assigned to a two- to three-year hitch at an embassy in a friendly country, for example. Sometimes their families have to stay behind, when they are stationed in a combat zone or other harsh environment.

Some CIA employees deploy on clandestine operations that they cannot reveal to anybody. They could be assigned for months or even years at a time to a mission that they can never explain to their spouses and children. This requires extreme devotion to duty for all concerned. Military personnel often have to deploy for long periods of time but they can usually stay in touch with their families through the internet, care packages and telephone calls. CIA operatives sometimes have to walk out the door with no explanation at all, knowing that they will not be able to contact their loved ones until they have returned from the mission. Even then, they will not be able to talk about their adventures with their family. It should come as no surprise that many CIA employees marry other CIA employees.

Do not let the prospect of long deployments stop you from pursuing a career with the CIA. Nobody will force you to spend your entire career in a job that requires this lifestyle, but make sure to seize the opportunity when you are still relatively young and do not have family concerns.

DESCRIPTION OF THE WORK

Application Process

No matter what job you aspire to do for the CIA you will have to go through a lengthy application process. The nature of the CIA's work demands that it take its time reviewing applications for employment in order to make sure it only hires careerists worthy of the enormous trust that will be placed in them. The entire process, from submitting an application to completing the background investigation can take anywhere from two months to a full year.

Go to www.cia.gov and take a look at the available positions. You may apply for four positions at a time. The application will ask all the usual questions about your education and work history, but will also delve into questions you will not find on most job applications, like foreign language proficiency, foreign cultural sensitivity, time spent overseas and military experience. The application will also ask questions about brushes with the law, drug use and credit history. Answer honestly. If you are selected for a position, the agency will conduct an exhaustive background investigation and get to the truth anyway. It is always better to be honest than to get caught in a lie.

The CIA tries to respond to applicants within 45 days. Due to the huge volume of applications it receives, however, the agency stipulates that if you do not hear from them within that time frame it is because they will not be offering you an interview. This does not mean you should not apply again. If something significant in your life changes, like earning a new degree or gaining relevant work experience, start the process all over again. Many CIA employees did not make it on their first try.

National Clandestine Service – Core Collectors

The CIA is most famous for its National Clandestine Service. These are the spies who gather intelligence on behalf of the United States. Do not bother to look for the word "spy" in any of the CIA's official job descriptions. It creates thorny legal problems, so the agency does not use this term. In fact, you should not even tell anybody anything about your plans to apply for a job with the CIA. Doing so may limit your future opportunities.

Clandestine operators are known as core collectors. Their job is to spot, assess, develop, recruit and handle individuals with access to foreign intelligence. This is the basis of human intelligence collection. Contrary to popular belief, HUMINT collectors rarely gather the intelligence themselves, through James Bond-style heroics. Most HUMINT is gathered from willing sources who volunteer to share what they know with core collectors.

Core collectors serve undercover. That means they are often supplied with a false identity and job to conceal their actions. Core collectors may or may not be able to bring their families with them on overseas assignments. Core collectors work in teams, but must be able to work without supervision, and in an environment in which circumstances can change instantly and there often is nobody to ask what to do next.

There are two basic career paths for core collectors: operations officers and collection management officers. The CIA places careerists on one of these two paths based on their demonstrated strengths and weaknesses determined during the 18-month Clandestine Service Trainee program. Operations officers are full-time HUMINT collectors, while collection management officers oversee and facilitate collections. Both can expect to spend more than half of their careers in overseas positions.

Intelligence Analysis

Analysts are the backbone of any intelligence agency. Clandestine operators and technical specialists using incredibly sophisticated technology may get the credit for collecting information, but it is the analysts who turn it into actionable intelligence. Keep this in mind for your intelligence training: Information is just information. Information that has been subject to analysis is intelligence.

The 17 agencies of the United States Intelligence Community collect a huge amount of information. Only a very small amount of it ends up as actionable intelligence. Analysts sort through the stacks to cull the most important bits and turn them into something useful. Finished intelligence can take many forms, including short updates on important situations, lengthy and detailed reports, or briefs intended to be delivered to an audience. All of these products have the same purpose – to help leaders to make decisions. The results of the CIA's work help military and government leaders to guide their efforts in ways that will prove advantageous to the United States and its allies and interests.

The CIA employs analysts in many specialties, including counterterrorism, counterintelligence, military and political analysis, targeting analysis, crime and counternarcotics, psychological and psychiatric analysis, and medical analysis, among others. These professionals use a method known as all-source analysis to find the essential truth hidden in mounds of distraction. All-source analysis, as the name suggests, uses all available sources, classified and unclassified, to support analysis. This is a highly intellectual process.

Science, Engineering and Technology

The CIA uses a great deal of advanced technology to conduct its operations. The exact nature of that technology is not public knowledge. It clearly covers a very wide range, however, as the agency has positions for science, engineering and technology professionals of many varieties. The agency employs professionals in the fields of biology, chemistry, computer science, mathematics, physics and every kind of engineering discipline you can think of, including aerospace, electrical, mechanical, chemical and computer.

All science, engineering and technology officers work for the agency's Directorate of Science and Technology as technical intelligence officers, or TIOs. Several career paths are open to TIOs, including operations tradecraft, technical research, technical development and technical analysis. All specialties are ultimately devoted to providing the agency with the tools it needs to stay one step ahead of the competition.

Foreign Languages

The CIA justly prides itself on its foreign languages capabilities. Almost all CIA employees speak at least one language other than English, and many are fluent in several. The agency values foreign language proficiency so highly that it offers monetary incentives for employees to learn and maintain foreign languages. There is also a hiring bonus offered to applicants who already know a foreign language.

The CIA maintains its own language learning program, the Central Intelligence Language Institute, to train employees in critical foreign languages. All languages are valued, but some more than others. Spanish is valuable, for example, but Arabic, Chinese and Pashtu are more valuable because it is much harder to find fluent speakers of these languages, and because these languages are spoken in places where the CIA has the most pressing needs.

Open Source Officers

The value of a foreign language to a clandestine operator is obvious, but most CIA linguists work behind desks. Open source officers, for example, fill a critical role in intelligence analysis by analyzing foreign media and other publicly available information to find nuggets of data that may be important to American decision- makers. You can learn a lot by reading your adversary's newspapers and websites. Doing so requires not only fluency in a language, but familiarity with the associated country and culture. Many CIA linguists are first-generation Americans with strong links to their ancestral culture. Their insight is extremely valuable to the process of intelligence analysis.

In the years after the September 11, 2001 terrorist attacks on the United States, an al-Qaeda leader remarked that he could discover 80 percent of everything he needed to know about an adversary from open sources. Think about that the next time you post something on a social media site. One of the first things the CIA will do during a background investigation is look into the tracks you have left on the internet. If you are the type who posts constantly, giving away your daily routine and making clear your relationships with other people, you may not be the type of person the CIA will want to hire.

Business, Security and Information Technology

Business, security, and information technology careers are the supporting cast at the CIA. Like any other large organization, the CIA employs thousands of administrative personnel, human resources specialists, accountants, contract managers, and the like. All of these positions are a little different at the CIA, however. For starters, all CIA employees must pass a background check. Being an administrative assistant may not sound like a high-level job but CIA administrative assistants have access to secret papers and computer data, and need to maintain the proper clearances to look at them. The same goes for all other positions at the agency.

The agency's IT positions are in a league of their own. CIA networks are at constant risk of hacking by foreign governments and freelance troublemakers, making data security of the utmost importance. The agency also needs top-notch geographers and cartographers, engineers, architects, and librarians, to name a few. There are thousands of career opportunities at the CIA that do not directly involve intelligence.

CIA PROFESSIONALS TALK ABOUT THEIR CAREERS

I Am a Clandestine Operations Core Collector

"I can't share very many details about what I do. I can tell you that this job is the most interesting, exciting and rewarding thing I've ever done.

I majored in political science in college, with a minor in one of the CIA's critical languages. I wasn't sure I was headed to the CIA after college, but I knew I wanted to get into international affairs and learning a critical language seemed like an excellent way to get a leg up on the competition.

It took a little more than a year for the CIA and me to jump through all the hoops necessary to put me on the payroll. The background investigation was exhaustive, with multiple polygraph screenings, searches of my finances, travel history, and personal and professional associations. There are many levels of security clearances, but as a core collector I had to be vetted for all of them.

Finally, the day came to start the Clandestine Service Trainee Program, the rigorous, 18-month ordeal that prepares CIA careerists for duty in the field. It was extremely demanding, and a number of people dropped out. The CIA asks a lot of its core collectors. To say that this job isn't for everybody would be a gross understatement.

I have spent about two-thirds of my career stationed overseas. In simple terms, my job is to locate and recruit people who have access to foreign intelligence of interest to the United States. Contrary to popular belief, core collectors are not really spies. Our main function is to find people who already have valuable information and inspire them to share it with us voluntarily. The overwhelming majority of human intelligence is gathered from willing volunteers, many of whom share their knowledge at great personal risk. This is the main reason why we operate undercover. Our sources may risk their lives to tell us things we need to know. We do everything in our power to protect them.

I like my job because it puts me on the front lines of the geopolitical battles always raging just below the events that make the news. It comes with many sacrifices, like not being able to tell my family what I've been up to all day, and occasional long separations from loved ones, but the mission is very valuable to the nation. I'm glad to be a part of it."

I Am a Science and Technology Analyst

"It used to be relatively easy to keep tabs on scientific and technological developments being pursued by our adversaries. There was really only one adversary worth keeping an eye on throughout the Cold War – the Soviet Union. The world has become much more complicated since then.

We not only monitor scientific and technological progress being made by nation-state adversaries like Iran or North Korea, but by non-state actors like the various al-Qaeda factions spread out across the Middle East, Central Asia and North Africa. They don't really develop technology, but they do acquire and deploy it, and sometimes in ingenious ways. The improvised explosive device, or IED, that proved so devastating against American and allied troops in Afghanistan was a clever adaptation of pretty standard bombs and cell phones. Defeating something so simple proved to be very difficult.

I have a master's degree in physics, and I joined the CIA after a few years of doing research for a very large industrial company. I enjoyed my old job but it lacked a spark, a mission focus that could keep my interest. That's when I looked into the CIA. I was interested to learn that they employ many people with skills like mine, and sometimes for jobs you wouldn't think of.

I'm not a science officer, I'm a science analyst. There's a difference. The CIA's science officers develop new tools to help the CIA conduct its mission. As an analyst I use my scientific knowledge to analyze the scientific progress being made by a wide variety of adversaries. I've spent parts of my career specializing in nuclear proliferation, energy security, and conventional weapons systems. Nuclear proliferation has been the most compelling assignment for me.

I have spent essentially all of my career at Langley, although I've been able to take some very interesting trips to places I never thought I'd go. That, I think, is the key to a career at the CIA. You get to explore topics and places that you never dreamed about."

I Am an Open Source Officer

"It never ceases to amaze me how many people are so quick to dismiss open-source intelligence. They think that anything that isn't classified can't be very important. Nothing could be further from the truth. Open-source intelligence is the context for everything else.

Let me give you an example. Everybody knows that the United States does not get along with North Korea. The CIA and other intelligence agencies do their best to stay on top of the latest developments in that police state. Open sources guide many of their efforts. When the North Korean leader makes a public proclamation, the intelligence agencies scramble to get to the details behind it. The first thing they need is a careful analysis of the public proclamation. Who reported it? When and where did the leader make it? What subtle cultural clues may be lurking in the specific language or even gestures he used while it was being made? Where does this proclamation fit into North Korea's larger geopolitical strategy? None of these pieces is classified, but when they are pulled together and subject to analysis, they paint a very telling picture that can be used to guide the efforts of other intelligence collectors.

Newspapers, television, radio, websites, unclassified

government documents, can all be helpful to an enemy. They are also easy to manipulate. Contrary to popular belief, the internet has not completely brought down the walls between countries and cultures. The architecture of the internet gives websites you visit your location. If you are in the United States your computer will relay this information to websites, even if you have taken steps to obscure your exact location. Many websites tailor their information to the audience. If you are sitting in the United States you may get one version of the news while somebody logging on from, say, Iran will get another version, even though it's on the same website. Part of my job is to sort through the obfuscation in order to stay abreast of who is sending what messages to whom.

I learned my skills during a five-year hitch as an intelligence officer in the Navy. I majored in history and minored in a critical language in college, then spent a few years traveling in the region where that language is spoken, before joining the Navy. When I got to the end of my five-year obligation in the Navy, I decided to check out career opportunities with other intelligence agencies. I figured I would stay in the Navy if nothing else turned up, but the CIA offered me a job very quickly, based on my military experience and language proficiency."

I Am a Research Scientist

"The CIA uses the best technology there is to accomplish its mission. The Directorate of Science and Technology employs scientists and engineers in every discipline you can imagine in order to keep the agency and the nation it serves one step ahead of everyone else.

I never set out to work for the CIA. I earned a PhD in chemistry over a very long period of time, earning my bachelor's, master's and doctoral degrees at different universities, and completing internships and research fellowships with several organizations. I also traveled extensively, and spent a few stretches working overseas in various capacities. By the time I finished my doctorate, I had turned myself into an excellent candidate for the CIA without even knowing it.

The CIA recognized it, however. Let's just say that a friend of a friend called somebody, who sent an email to somebody else, whose associates got in touch with me. It still took almost a year to get through the hiring process.

I can't tell you exactly what I do. What I can say is that I compare favorably to Q, the genius inventor from the James Bond movies who issues the latest and greatest gadgets to 007 before he deploys on a mission. My work is challenging, and it can be fun.

I'd recommend this job to any scientist who wants to take an unconventional path, delve into science on the cutting edge, and serve the country at the same time. There really is no career quite like a career with the CIA."

I Am a Paramilitary Operations Officer

"I spent 10 years in Army special forces before I came to the CIA. There is only one path to a career as a paramilitary operations officer at the CIA, and that's through the military.

I earned a bachelor's degree in psychology before joining the Army. I started out as an infantry officer and transitioned into special operating forces, or SOF, as soon as I could. Along the way I learned a critical language at the military's Defense Language Institute in Monterey, California. To me, SOF is really at the tip of the spear. We traveled around the world to conduct our missions. They were all vitally important to national security, and the public didn't even know anything about what we were doing to protect them.

I joined the CIA after the Army because I wanted to ease into something a little more subtle than kicking down doors. I joined the CIA through a special program intended to transition military personnel into CIA careers as expeditiously as possible. Security clearances and other formalities can be taken care of pretty easily when the military and CIA work together and hand off responsibility in an orderly manner. It's just one of many good reasons to do a hitch in the military before heading to the CIA.

All CIA paramilitary operations officers complete the 18-month Clandestine Service Trainee program. We use our specialized military skills to protect CIA assets in the field, and to collect our own intelligence. We are not truly a military force, and are prohibited by law from wearing military uniforms, but we can do some of the same things when we need to.

This job isn't for everybody, and there's only one way to get it. The military isn't for everybody, either. It's a great way to get started in life, even if you don't move into a related field. You'll learn things in uniform that you can't learn anywhere else."

PERSONAL QUALIFICATIONS

IT SHOULD BE CLEAR THAT NOT JUST anybody can work for the CIA. Just getting hired is difficult enough, but succeeding and rising through the ranks are even harder.

In order to succeed at the CIA careerists must do well academically. That is about more than just getting good grades or high test scores. It means having real enthusiasm for intellectual work. Intelligence analysis is equal parts fascination and routine. The idea is to subject information from many different sources to a rigorous analytical process in order to produce finished intelligence. There are many ways to go about this process, some of which are very complex. The CIA supports its employees with a full slate of training programs and seminars designed to keep them abreast of the latest methods and tools. Even employees who do not deal directly with intelligence analysis need to be comfortable working in an environment characterized by constant intellectual inquiry. The information never stops flowing at the CIA.

Self-confidence is another key quality you will need. The CIA attracts the best graduates from top universities and the military. These people are smart, competitive and not afraid to make their opinions known. Intellectuals like to argue, and debate the issues. Not in a mean-spirited way, but because commitment is the key to getting your ideas across to other people. You will not need to go into work every day with your guard up, but you will need to be prepared to stand up for yourself, your beliefs, and your work.

The CIA's primary mission is to provide intelligence to senior decision-makers. Almost everything produced by the agency is a joint effort. Nothing goes straight from an analyst to the president, for example. Reports are generally written and edited by a team of analysts, approved by supervisors and sent up the chain of command until they reach the top. Not everything that goes into the first draft will make it into the final report. If you contribute an idea to a project you may have to fight to keep it in, and accept it gracefully when it is cut.

Most importantly, careerists who want to survive at the CIA need to be absolutely devoted to their duty. Your devotion needs to start now. If you want to get hired, you need to have a virtually flawless personal history. No police record, no debt or money problems, no history of alcohol or drug abuse, no personal or professional associations with people or organizations of questionable character. Everybody who is hired by the CIA is hired pending the results of a background investigation. A background issue can stop the hiring process even if the agency wants you.

After you start work, your devotion to duty will be tested every day. You will be granted a security clearance that gives you access to classified intelligence. You will not be able to discuss your work with people who are not cleared to know about it. That means you will not be able to chat about work during dinner with your family. Normal people can do that, but your world will be anything but normal if you pursue a career with the CIA. You will not be able to tell your family why you will be away on a "business trip," or where you are going, or for how long. You may be asked to assume great personal risk, especially if you pursue a career in clandestine operations. If you succeed, you may be awarded a medal that you cannot take home and cannot even tell anybody about. If you fail, you could be memorialized on a wall at Langley covered with stars – one for each CIA employee killed in the line of duty. There are no names on that wall. Nobody will ever know who you were or what you did. That is extreme devotion.

ATTRACTIVE FEATURES

THE CIA EMPLOYS MANY SMART, intellectually gifted people to do very complex and interesting jobs. The kind of people who can do anything they want and who could probably make more money working in the private sector. The members of the CIA community love what they do or they would not be doing it. If you share this passion, if you are insatiably curious, love to dig into exhaustive research, are interested in world affairs, and are absolutely certain that you are on the right side, you would have a hard time finding a place where you could be more fulfilled.

You will find satisfaction in knowing how the world really works. CIA employees do not have front-row seats to history in the making, they have backstage passes. If you pursue a career with the agency, you will be on the inside track on everything that is really happening. You will discover that even the best news media reports do no uncover what you and your colleagues know. Some things you learn you may find disturbing. The world is a more violent and hostile place than you probably think. The game of geopolitics is complicated and ruthless, and you will have a role to play in it. It is fair to say that every industry or profession has its own secrets, but it is surely true to say that the CIA has more interesting secrets than most.

The CIA is the world's premier intelligence agency. There are a handful of other national intelligence agencies of real consequence, particularly Britain's MI6, Russia's FSB and Israel's Mossad, but none comes close to the CIA for the sheer breadth and depth of its operations. You will have opportunities to do things in your job that you could not possibly do anywhere else. Some will be thrilling, some may be surprisingly routine, but they will all be very, very interesting.

UNATTRACTIVE FEATURES

A CAREER WITH THE CIA HAS A FEW downsides, chief among them, the need for secrecy. A security clearance is an enormous responsibility. As a CIA employee you will be granted a security clearance that gives you access to classified intelligence. You will undergo a very thorough background investigation. Investigators will interview you, members of your family, former employers and anybody else they think may be able to shed some light on your trustworthiness. Everything about you, your family, your past, and your present, will be scrutinized, from parking tickets on up. This process will repeat itself every five years, and maybe more often than that, depending upon your mission. It is not a pleasant process, but it is easy compared to the need for constant secrecy. Unlike most people, you will not be able to come home from work and talk about what you did that day. You may be able to discuss a few mundane topics like office birthday parties and the like, but you will never be able to tell your family exactly what you do, or even where you have been. Even if your job title is unclassified and comes with an unclassified description, you will never be able to get into any details about what you do or how you do it. This can put a serious strain on personal relationships, especially with the people closest to you.

Not everybody thinks the CIA is as great as you think it is. In fact, many people like to think of the CIA as a criminal organization with blood on its hands. It would not be possible to count the number of conspiracy theories tied to the CIA and its supposed covert actions over the years, from gun-running in Nicaragua to drug-dealing in Afghanistan. Everything the CIA does is regulated by law and subject to oversight by Congress. Every few years a member of Congress decides to start a formal investigation into some allegation of wrongdoing, and the agency is always exonerated. Every once in a while a CIA employee gets fired for making a few bad decisions, but that is hardly evidence of a systemic conspiracy. The CIA is a large agency, distributed around the world, and it is not perfect. Some people are determined to assume the worst. Be prepared to be snubbed, shunned and feared.

Not by everybody, of course, and not even by most people. Of course, not many people will even know that you work for the CIA.

You should also be aware of the fact that not everybody is suited for government work. All government jobs are subject to artificial strictures, innumerable rules and endless politics. All government employees have a civilian rank according to the General Schedule, from GS-1 to GS-15. Promotions are often made for reasons of seniority rather than merit. Knowledge, experience, and accomplishments are not necessarily the criteria to move up in the organization. Government agencies are very political. Although the CIA is officially nonpartisan, it takes orders from elected officials who are very partisan. Orders can change at any time, and sometimes for reasons that have very little to do with maintaining national security.

EDUCATION AND TRAINING

TECHNICALLY, BACHELOR'S DEGREES are only required for careerists seeking overseas positions. As a practical matter, however, you should plan on college if you hope to compete. The CIA does not require aspiring careerists to earn a degree in any particular subject. The agency employs professionals in so many areas of expertise it would be impossible to recommend any one major. A foreign language is a must, with Chinese and Arabic in particularly high demand.

Analysts earn degrees in liberal arts subjects like history, sociology, psychology, political science, and even strategic intelligence, a specialized degree offered by a few universities. The agency also employs many information technology professionals with degrees in every possible specialty within computer science. There are also engineers and scientists. You have a wide latitude when it comes to choosing a major for a career in intelligence.

The most important thing you can do while you are in college is distinguish yourself academically. Competition for CIA jobs is incredibly tough and mediocre grades are unacceptable. Spend a year studying abroad and learning a foreign language. Sign up to be a research assistant for a professor working on an interesting project. Win an essay contest. Do anything you can do to distinguish yourself academically.

Definitely complete an internship while you are in college. An internship is a full-time job that takes the place of classes for a summer or semester. Most internships are paid, and all come with opportunities you cannot get even as a regular employee, like specialized seminars designed for interns and access to high-ranking people who take an interest in the up-and-coming generation.

It is very common for recent graduates to find their first real jobs with the same organization where they did their internship. An internship provides a very valuable glimpse into the career you think you want to enter. Do not miss this opportunity.

The CIA offers internships, as do most of the other agencies in the intelligence community. An internship in a related agency like the Department of State or the Department of Defense will also give you valuable insight and enhance your résumé.

Internships with federal agencies are extremely competitive. Those with intelligence agencies will require you to pass a background check. If you want to get into an intelligence profession, you have to start walking the straight and narrow right now.

An excellent way to get some experience for a career with the CIA is to do a hitch in the military. All of the services have their own intelligence operations, and they all interact with the CIA. A few years in the military will get you a security clearance and hands-on experience you cannot get anywhere else. This experience will serve you well when the time comes to compete for sought-after openings at the CIA. You can enlist out of high school and use the GI Bill to pay for college after you get out, or you can apply for a commission as an officer after college. The Reserve Officer Training Corps, or ROTC, can pay for some or all of your college expenses. The military is not for everybody, but even a single, five-year hitch will open many doors later in your career. If you join the CIA you will be working with military personnel for your entire career. Look into the opportunities offered by the military.

A graduate degree may be a necessity later in your career. Most CIA employees have a master's degree, and many earn PhDs. The subject of your degree will probably be determined by your career path. You can also plan to earn an advanced degree shortly after finishing your undergraduate work, but be sure to fit in some practical experience along the way.

EARNINGS

THE CIA PAYS ITS EMPLOYEES ACCORDING to the General Schedule, the pay and allowances system that covers most federal employees. Commonly known simply as "GS," the General Schedule spells out pay scales and creates a rank system for federal civilian employees.

The GS is divided into 15 grades, each of which has 10 steps. Federal employees often refer to themselves by their grade and step, as in "I'm an 11/7. My boss is a 13/10." It is the same thing as military personnel referring to themselves and their colleagues by rank: "I'm a lieutenant. My boss is a commander." In fact, the 15 grades in the GS align with the 15 military ranks below admiral and general. This is helpful in environments in which military personnel and civilians work together, because everybody knows who outranks whom.

The GS is fairly flexible, and starting salaries are not necessarily written in stone. You will find job announcements stating that the job in question starts at, for example, $50,790 per year to $57,562 per year. That means it starts somewhere between Grade 11, Step 1 and Grade 11, Step 5. Steps and grades are determined by the rank and difficulty of the job, and by the credentials and experience of the employee.

The GS currently goes from a low of about $18,000 per year for a 1/1, to about $130,000 for a 15/10. Most CIA jobs for recent college graduates will start at the GS-9, at least, and maybe as high as GS-13 for careerists with advanced degrees, military experience or critical languages. The GS-9 grade starts at almost $42,000 per year, and maxes out at almost $55,000. The GS-13 grade starts at about $72,000 per year and rises to almost $95,000. To see the entire General schedule go to the Federal Office of Personnel Management at www.opm.gov

Like all federal agencies, the CIA adjusts its pay scale for high-cost areas. Luckily CIA employees, Washington, DC is a very high-cost area. That means that the salaries for CIA employees stationed in Langley is higher than the standard GS would suggest. CIA employees stationed overseas are also paid additional allowances. The CIA even offers overtime for some positions. The details are available at www.cia.gov

A few thousand federal employees hold a rank above GS-15. These employees are paid according to the Senior Executive Service schedule and are commonly known as SESs. SESs are the civilian equivalents of generals or admirals. Pay for SESs ranges from a minimum of $120,000 to a maximum of about $180,000. The director of the CIA is paid according to the Executive Schedule for the highest-ranking government employees. In a recent year, that schedule topped out at $200,000 per year.

OPPORTUNITIES

WHETHER YOU ARE ENTERING A career in the CIA at an opportune time depends upon how you look at it. The world has become a much more dangerous place since the end of the Cold War. The threats to the United States and its interests have multiplied many times since the demise of the Soviet Union, and most of those threats are hidden in the shadows. Unlike the Soviet Union, al-Qaeda does not hold well-publicized military parades and march around in uniforms.

Addressing the threats of the current era requires a corps of resolute, innovative patriots willing and able to get inside the minds of America's adversaries and head off threats before they become actions. The CIA, like all of the agencies in the Intelligence Community, has seen significant growth in recent years to meet this challenge. Even while Washington has reduced funding for other agencies involved in foreign relations, like the Departments of State and Defense, intelligence agencies have grown because they deliver invaluable results. In that sense, there has been no better time to look into a career with the CIA.

Once you are in, you can move up by expanding your skills and credentials, and by volunteering for hard jobs. The CIA is a very academic agency, offering courses on a huge variety of topics, and encouraging its employees to seek out additional education. There are many opportunities for agency employees to take advantage of tuition-reimbursement programs to minimize the cost of earning an additional degree.

Picking up a third or fourth language will definitely be a plus.

Stepping up for the hard jobs will really accelerate the pace of your career. Even if you are not a clandestine operator, you can still volunteer for jobs in remote places where few people want to go. This may require some sacrifices, such as leaving your family behind for a year or so, or being largely confined to an embassy compound in a dangerous country. You may even have to live in a tent in a combat zone. Many CIA employees served alongside military personnel in Afghanistan and Iraq, for example, and several were killed in the line of duty. There are many agencies in Washington in which seniority and simply not making any big mistakes are enough to propel someone up the ladder. The CIA is not like that. If you want to get ahead, plan to step outside your comfort zone.

GETTING STARTED

YOU SHOULD START THE CIA APPLICATION process while you are still in your last year of college or military service. The process is long and convoluted and can take more than a year. Depending upon the backlog of background investigations, you may not be able to walk through the doors at Langley until a year after you have been offered a job.

Get your personal marketing materials together. The CIA requires applicants to submit a résumé. Your résumé will be scrutinized by a computer before it ever gets to human hands, so make sure to read job descriptions carefully and use keywords from the descriptions in your résumé to make sure you catch the computer's eye. Even if you make it through the computer's first look at your résumé, it will probably be viewed by a human being for less than a minute before going into the tall stack of rejects or the much shorter stack of applicants to call for an interview. There are many books and software applications available to help you write a first-class résumé. You can also hire a professional résumé writer.

Make sure you have a few references lined up who can vouch for your abilities and trustworthiness. A couple of professors, or a former employer or two. Better yet, a former supervisor from the CIA or other intelligence agency or government agency where you did your internship. Washington is a very small place in which people who are well-connected tend to get the best jobs. Make sure the people you list as references are aware of the fact that somebody from the CIA may be contacting them. Other than that, however, you should keep your plans to yourself. Telling the world that you are applying for a job at the world's largest intelligence agency is a poor way to show that you can keep a secret.

Most of all, do not lose faith. Many CIA employees apply multiple times before they are finally hired. Others apply to multiple intelligence agencies. If they do not land anything at the CIA, maybe they will end up at the Defense Intelligence Agency or the National Security Agency. If you have the skills and determination to make the world a little safer, there will be a place for you somewhere. Good luck.

ASSOCIATIONS
PERIODICALS
WEBSITES

■ **Bond, James Bond**
www.007.com

■ **Central Intelligence Agency**
www.cia.gov

■ **Council on Foreign Relations**
www.cfr.org

■ **Defense Intelligence Agency**
www.dia.mil

■ **Department of Energy**
www.energy.gov

■ **Department of Homeland Security**
www.dhs.gov

■ **Department of State**
www.state.gov

■ **Drug Enforcement Administration**
www.dea.gov

■ **Economist**
www.economist.com

■ **Federal Bureau of Investigation**
www.fbi.gov

■ **Foreign Affairs**
www.foreignaffairs.com

■ **Foreign Policy**
www.foreignpolicy.com

■ **Institute of World Politics**
www.iwp.edu

- **Jane's**
www.janes.com
- **National Geospatial Intelligence Agency**
www.nga.mil
- **National Reconnaissance Office**
www.nro.gov
- **National Security Agency**
www.nsa.gov
- **Office of the Director of National Intelligence**
www.odni.gov
- **Secret Intelligence Service**
www.sis.gov.uk
- **Strategic Forecasting**
www.stratfor.com
- **United States Air Force**
www.airforce.com
- **United States Army**
www.army.com
- **United States Coast Guard**
www.gocoastguard.com
- **United States Intelligence Community**
www.intelligence.gov
- **United States Marine Corps**
www.marines.com
- **United States Navy**
www.navy.com

Institute For Career Research

Website www.careers-internet.org

For information on other Careers Reports please contact

info@careers-internet.org

Made in the USA
Middletown, DE
14 August 2017